Air Fryer Gr

2021

Discover how simple and quick you
can prepare juicy, healthy and
delicious dishes for the whole family
to fry, grill, bake, and bake

Nancy Cooke

TABLE OF CONTENTS

INTRODUCTION

Thank you for purchasing the best cookbook to cook with the Power XL Air Fryer!

Imagine having foods with less oil, fat and calories while presenting the delicious taste and texture of your favorite foods. The air fryer has an internal die-cast aluminum grill, has a deep fryer and external grill / rotisserie, together create a perfect cooking combination.

To conquer all palates, use this fantastic tool and follow the recipes in this book. I'm sure you'll make a great impression !!

Enjoy your meal !!

BREAKFAST

1. Breakfast Egg Tomato

Preparation Time: 10 Minutes

Cooking Time: 24 Minutes

Servings: 2

Ingredients:

- 2 eggs
- 2 large fresh tomatoes
- 1 tsp fresh parsley
- Pepper
- Salt

Directions:

1. Preheat the air fryer to 325 F.
2. Cut off the top of a tomato and spoon out the tomato innards.
3. Break the egg in each tomato and place it in the air fryer basket and cook for 24 minutes.
4. Season with parsley, pepper, and salt.
5. Serve and enjoy.

Nutrition: Calories 95, Fat 5 g, Carbohydrates 7.5 g, Sugar 5.1 g, Protein 7 g, Cholesterol 164 mg

2. Mushroom Leek Frittata

Preparation Time: 10 Minutes

Cooking Time: 32 Minutes

Servings: 4

Ingredients:

- 6 eggs
- 6 oz mushrooms, sliced
- 1 cup leeks, sliced
- Salt

Directions:

1. Preheat the air fryer to 325 F.

2. Heat another pan over medium heat. Spray pan with cooking spray.

3. Add mushrooms, leeks, and salt in a pan sauté for 6 minutes.

4. Break eggs in a bowl and whisk well.

5. Transfer sautéed mushroom and leek mixture into the prepared baking dish.

6. Pour egg over mushroom mixture.

7. Put it in the air fryer then cook for 32 minutes.

8. Serve and enjoy.

Nutrition: Calories 116, Fat 7 g, Carbohydrates 5.1 g, Sugar 2.1 g, Protein 10 g, Cholesterol 245 mg

3. Perfect Breakfast Frittata

Preparation Time: 10 Minutes

Cooking Time: 32 Minutes

Servings: 2

Ingredients:

- 3 eggs
- 2 tbsp parmesan cheese, grated
- 2 tbsp sour cream
- 1/2 cup bell pepper, chopped
- 1/4 cup onion, chopped
- 1/2 tsp pepper
- 1/2 tsp salt

Directions:

1. Add eggs in a mixing bowl and whisk with the remaining ingredients.
2. Spray air fryer baking dish with cooking spray.
3. Pour egg mixture into the prepared dish and place it in the air fryer and cook at 350 F for 5 minutes.
4. Serve and enjoy.

Nutrition: Calories 227, Fat 15.2 g, Carbohydrates 6 g, Sugar 2.6 g, Protein 18.2 g, Cholesterol 271 mg

4. Indian Cauliflower

Preparation Time: 10 Minutes

Cooking Time: 20 Minutes

Servings: 2

Ingredients:

- 3 cups cauliflower florets
- 2 tbsp water
- 2 tsp fresh lemon juice
- ½ tbsp ginger paste
- 1 tsp chili powder
- ¼ tsp turmeric
- ½ cup vegetable stock
- Salt and Pepper

Directions:

1. Add all fixings into the air fryer baking dish and mix well.

2. Put it in the air fryer then cook at 400 F for 10 minutes.

3. Stir well and cook at 360 F for 10 minutes more.

4. Stir well and serve.

Nutrition: Calories 49, Fat 0.5 g, Carbohydrates 9 g, Sugar 3 g, Protein 3 g, Cholesterol 0 mg

5. Zucchini Salad

Preparation Time: 10 Minutes

Cooking Time: 25 Minutes

Servings: 4

Ingredients:

- 1 lb. zucchini, cut into slices
- 2 tbsp tomato paste
- ½ tbsp tarragon, chopped
- 1 yellow squash, diced
- ½ lb. carrots, peeled and diced
- 1 tbsp olive oil
- Pepper
- Salt

Directions:

1. In air fryer baking dish mix together zucchini, tomato paste, tarragon, squash, carrots, pepper, and salt. Drizzle with olive oil.
2. Put it in the air fryer then cook at 400 F for 25 minutes. Stir halfway through.
3. Serve and enjoy.

Nutrition: Calories 79, Fat 3 g, Carbohydrates 11 g, Sugar 5 g, Protein 2 g, Cholesterol 0 mg

6. Breakfast Frittata

Preparation Time: 5 Minutes

Cooking Time: 15 Minutes

Servings: 3

Ingredients:

- Six eggs
- 8 halved cherry tomatoes
- 2 tbsps. shredded parmesan cheese
- 1 Italian sausage, diced
- Salt and pepper

Directions:

1. Adjust the air fryer to 355 F.
2. Add the tomatoes and sausage to the baking dish.
3. Place the baking dish into the air fryer and cook for 5 minutes.
4. Meanwhile, add eggs, cheese, salt, oil, and pepper into the mixing bowl, then whisk properly.
5. Remove the baking dish from the air fryer and pour the egg mixture on top. Ensure you spread it evenly.

6. Place the dish back into the air fryer and bake for an additional 5 minutes.
7. Remove from air fryer and slice into wedges and serve.

Nutrition: Calories: 273 kcal Total Fat: 8.2g Carbs: 7g Protein: 14.2g

7. Morning Mini Cheeseburger Sliders

Preparation Time: 5 Minutes

Cooking Time: 10 Minutes

Servings: 6

Ingredients:

- 1 lb. ground beef
- Six slices of cheddar cheese
- Six dinner rolls
- Salt and Black pepper

Directions:

1. Adjust the air fryer to 390 F.
2. Form 6 beef patties (each about 2.5 oz.) and season with salt and black pepper.
3. Add the burger patties to the cooking basket and cook them for 10 minutes.
4. Remove the burger patties from the air fryer; place the cheese on top of burgers, return to the air fryer and cook for another minute.
5. Remove and put burgers on dinner rolls and serve warm.

Nutrition: Calories 262 kcal Total Fat: 9.4gCarbs: 8.2g Protein: 16.2g

8. Spanish Omelet

Preparation Time: 5 Minutes

Cooking Time: 15 Minutes

Servings: 2

Ingredients:

- Three eggs
- Cayenne or black pepper
- ½ cup finely chopped vegetables of your choosing.

Directions:

1. In a pan on high heat, stir-fry the vegetables in extra virgin olive oil until lightly crispy.
2. Cook the eggs with one tablespoon of water and a pinch of pepper.
3. When almost cooked, top with the vegetables and flip to cook briefly.
4. Serve

Nutrition: Calories 321 Fat 3 g Fiber 8 g Carbs 22 g Protein 16 g

9. Sausage Quiche

Preparation Time: 10 Minutes

Cooking Time: 25 Minutes

Servings: 4

Ingredients:

- 12 large eggs
- 1 cup heavy cream
- 1 tsp black pepper
- 12 oz sugar-free breakfast sausage
- 2 cups shredded cheddar cheese

Directions:

1. Preheat your fryer to 375°F/190°C.
2. Mix the eggs, heavy cream, salad, and pepper.
3. Add the breakfast sausage and cheddar cheese.
4. Pour the combination into a greased casserole saucer.
5. Bake for 25 minutes.
6. Cut into 12 squares and serve hot.

Nutrition: Calories 333 Fat 21.6 g Carbohydrates 30.1 g Sugar 2.3 g Protein 7.3 g Cholesterol 12 mg

MAINS: BEEF

1. Beef Curry

Preparation Time: 6 Minutes

Cooking Time: 44 Minutes

Servings: 4

Ingredients:

- 2 lb. beef (cut into cubes)
- 2 tbsp. tomato sauce
- 3 medium potatoes (cut into cubes)
- 2 yellow onions chopped
- 2 tbsp. olive oil
- 1 tbsp. wine mustard
- 2 garlic cloves (minced)
- 2-1/2 tbsp. curry
- 10 oz. can coconut milk
- Salt and black pepper to taste

Directions:

1. Preheat the air fryer to 3600F.
2. Place a pan over medium heat (make sure the pan fits into your air fryer), add oil, and heat until

shimmering. Add the onions and garlic, cook for 4 minutes or until translucent. Add the beef, curry powder, tomato sauce, coconut milk, salt, and pepper.

3. Stir and transfer to the air fryer; set the time for 40 minutes.

4. Serve and enjoy.

Nutrition: Calories: 231kcal, Fat: 15g, Carb: 20g, Proteins: 27g

2. Garlic and Bell Pepper Beef

Preparation Time: 30 Minutes

Cooking Time: 21 Minutes

Servings: 4

Ingredients:

- 11 oz. steak fillets (sliced)
- 1/2 cup beef stock
- 2 tbsp. olive oil
- 2 tbsp. fish sauce
- 4 cloves garlic (pressed)
- 1 red pepper (cut into thin strips)
- 4 green onions (sliced)
- 1 tbsp. sugar
- 2 tsp. corn flour
- Black pepper to taste

Directions:

1. In a pan, add beef, oil, garlic, black pepper, and bell pepper, stir, cover, and keep in the refrigerator for 30 minutes.

2. Preheat the air fryer to 3600F.

3. Put the pan to the air fryer and cook for 14 minutes. In a bowl, mix sugar and fish sauce, pour over the beef and cook for an additional 7 minutes.

4. Serve and enjoy.

Nutrition: Calories: 243kcal, Fat: 3g, Carb: 24g, Proteins: 38g

3. Beef and Green Onion Marinade

Preparation Time: 10 Minutes

Cooking Time: 20 Minutes

Servings: 4

Ingredients:

- 1 lb. lean beef
- 1 cup of soy sauce
- 5 garlic cloves (minced)
- 1/4 cup sesame seeds
- 1/2 cup of water
- 1 tsp. black pepper
- 1/4 cup brown sugar
- 1 cup green onion

Directions:

1. In a bowl, add soy sauce, onions, sugar, water, garlic, sesame seed, and pepper, whisk. Add the beef and toss to coat, leave for 10 minutes.
2. Preheat the air fryer to 3900F, drain the beef, and transfer to the air fryer. Cook for 20 minutes.
3. Serve with salad and enjoy.

Nutrition: Calories: 329kcal, Fat: 8g, Carb: 24g, Proteins: 22g

MAINS: SEAFOOD

1. Soy and Ginger Shrimp

Preparation Time: 8 Minutes

Cooking Time: 10 Minutes

Servings: 4

Ingredients:

- 2 tablespoons olive oil
- 2 tablespoons scallions, finely chopped
- 2 cloves garlic, chopped
- 1 teaspoon fresh ginger, grated
- 1 tablespoon dry white wine
- 1 tablespoon balsamic vinegar
- 1/4 cup soy sauce
- 1 tablespoon sugar
- 1-pound shrimp
- Salt and ground black pepper, to taste

Directions:

1. Preparing the Ingredients. To make the marinade, warm the oil in a saucepan; cook all ingredients, except the shrimp, salt, and black pepper. Now, let it cool.

2. Marinate the shrimp, covered, at least an hour, in the refrigerator.
3. Air Frying. After that, bake the shrimp at 350 degrees F for 8 to 10 minutes (depending on the size), turning once or twice. Season prepared shrimp with salt and black pepper and serve right away.

Nutrition: Calories: 165 Carbs: 5.8 Fat: 4.5g Fiber: 0g

2. Crispy Cheesy Fish Fingers

Preparation Time: 10 Minutes

Cooking Time: 20 Minutes

Servings: 4

Ingredients:

- Large codfish filet, approximately 6-8 ounces, fresh or frozen and thawed, cut into 1 ½-inch strips
- 2 raw eggs
- ½ cup of breadcrumbs (we like Panko, but any brand or home recipe will do)
- 2 tablespoons of shredded or powdered parmesan cheese
- 1 tablespoons of shredded cheddar cheese
- Pinch of salt and pepper

Directions:

1. Preparing the Ingredients. Cover the basket of the XL air fryer oven with a lining of tin foil, leaving the edges uncovered to allow air to circulate through the basket.
2. Preheat the air fryer oven to 350 degrees.

3. In a large mixing bowl, beat the eggs until fluffy and until the yolks and whites are fully combined.
4. Dunk all the fish strips in the beaten eggs, fully submerging.
5. In a separate mixing bowl, combine the bread crumbs with the parmesan, cheddar, and salt and pepper, until evenly mixed.
6. One by one, coat the egg-covered fish strips in the mixed dry ingredients so that they're fully covered, and place on the foil-lined Oven rack/basket. Place the Rack on the middle-shelf of the XL air fryer oven.
7. Air Frying. Set the air-fryer timer to 20 minutes.
8. Halfway through the cooking time, shake the handle of the air-fryer so that the breaded fish jostles inside and fry-coverage is even.
9. After 20 minutes, when the fryer shuts off, the fish strips will be perfectly cooked and their breaded crust golden-brown and delicious! Using tongs, remove from the air fryer oven and set on a serving dish to cool.

Nutrition: Calories: 170 Carbs: 10g Fat: 4g Protein: 25g Fiber: 3g

3. Panko-Crusted Tilapia

Preparation Time: 5 Minutes

Cooking Time: 10 Minutes

Servings: 3

Ingredients:

- 2 tsp. Italian seasoning
- 2 tsp. lemon pepper
- 1/3 C. panko breadcrumbs
- 1/3 C. egg whites
- 1/3 C. almond flour
- 3 tilapia fillets
- Olive oil

Directions:

1. Preparing the Ingredients. Place panko, egg whites, and flour into separate bowls. Mix lemon pepper and Italian seasoning in with breadcrumbs.

2. Pat tilapia fillets dry. Dredge in flour, then egg, then breadcrumb mixture.

3. Air Frying. Add to the Oven rack/basket and spray lightly with olive oil. Place the Rack on the middle-shelf of the XL air fryer oven.

4. Cook 10-11 minutes at 400 degrees, making sure to flip halfway through cooking.

Nutrition: Calories: 256 Fat: 9g Protein: 39g Sugar: 5g

4. Fish Cake with Mango Relish

Preparation Time: 5 Minutes

Cooking Time: 10 Minutes

Servings: 4

Ingredients:

- 1 lb. White Fish Fillets
- 3 Tbsps. Ground Coconut
- 1 Ripened Mango
- ½ Tsps. Chili Paste
- Tbsps. Fresh Parsley
- 1 Green Onion
- 1 Lime
- 1 Tsp Salt
- 1 Egg

Directions:

1. Preparing the Ingredients. To make the relish, peel and dice the mango into cubes. Combine with a half teaspoon of chili paste, a tablespoon of parsley, and the zest and juice of half a lime.

2. In a food processor, pulse the fish until it forms a smooth texture. Place into a bowl and add the salt, egg, chopped green onion, parsley, two tablespoons of the coconut, and the remainder of the chili paste and lime zest and juice. Combine well
3. Portion the mixture into 10 equal balls and flatten them into small patties. Pour the reserved tablespoon of coconut onto a dish and roll the patties over to coat.
4. Preheat the Air fryer oven to 390 degrees
5. Air Frying. Place the fish cakes into the XL air fryer oven and cook for 8 minutes.
6. Serve hot with mango relish

Nutrition: Calories: 160 Carbs: 10g Fat: 4g Protein: 30g Fiber: 3g

5. Firecracker Shrimp

Preparation Time: 10 Minutes

Cooking Time: 8 Minutes

Servings: 4

Ingredients:

- 1-pound raw shrimp, peeled and deveined
- Salt
- Pepper
- 1 egg
- ½ cup all-purpose flour
- ¾ cup panko bread crumbs
- Cooking oil
- For the firecracker sauce
- 1/3 cup sour cream
- 2 tablespoons Sriracha
- ¼ cup sweet chili sauce

Directions:

1. Preparing the Ingredients. With salt and pepper, season the shrimp to taste. In a small bowl, beat the egg. In another small bowl, place the flour. In a third small bowl, add the panko bread crumbs.

2. Spray the Oven rack/basket with cooking oil. Dip the shrimp in the flour, then the egg, and then the bread crumbs. Place the shrimp in the Oven rack/basket. It is okay to stack them. Spray the shrimp with cooking oil. Place the Rack on the middle-shelf of the XL air fryer oven.

3. Air Frying. Cook for 4 minutes. Open the XL air fryer oven and flip the shrimp. I recommend flipping individually instead of shaking to keep the breading intact. Cook for extra 4 minutes or until crisp.

4. While the shrimp is cooking, make the firecracker sauce: In a small bowl, combine the sour cream, Sriracha, and sweet chili sauce. Mix well. Serve with the shrimp.

Nutrition: Calories: 266 Carbs: 23g Fat: 6g Protein: 27g Fiber: 1g

6. Sesame Seeds Coated Fish

Preparation Time: 10 Minutes

Cooking Time: 8 Minutes

Servings: 5

Ingredients:

- 3 tablespoons plain flour
- 2 eggs
- ½ cup sesame seeds, toasted
- ½ cup breadcrumbs
- 1/8 teaspoon dried rosemary, crushed
- Pinch of salt
- Pinch of black pepper
- 3 tablespoons olive oil
- 5 frozen fish fillets (white fish of your choice)

Directions:

1. Preparing the Ingredients. In a shallow dish, place flour. In another shallow dish, whisk the eggs. In a third shallow dish, add remaining ingredients except fish fillets and mix till a crumbly mixture form.

2. Coat the fillets with flour and shake off the excess flour.
3. Next, dip the fillets in the egg.
4. Then coat the fillets with sesame seeds mixture generously.
5. Preheat the XL air fryer oven to 390 degrees F.
6. Air Frying. Line an Air fryer rack/basket with a piece of foil. Arrange the fillets into prepared basket.
7. Cook for about 14 minutes, flipping once after 10 minutes.

Nutrition: Calories: 315 Fat: 1g Protein: 22g Fiber: 3g

MAINS: VEGETABLES

1. Quick Creamy Spinach

Preparation Time: 10 Minutes

Cooking Time: 15 Minutes

Servings: 2

Ingredients:

- 10 oz frozen spinach, thawed
- 1/4 cup parmesan cheese, shredded
- 1/2 tsp ground nutmeg
- 1 tsp pepper
- 4 oz cream cheese, diced
- 2 tsp garlic, minced
- 1 small onion, chopped
- 1 tsp salt

Directions:

1. Spray 6-inch pan with cooking spray and set aside.
2. In a bowl, mix together spinach, cream cheese, garlic, onion, nutmeg, pepper, and salt.
3. Pour spinach mixture into the prepared pan.

4. Place dish in air fryer basket and air fry at 350 F for 10 minutes.
5. Open air fryer basket and sprinkle parmesan cheese on top of spinach mixture and air fry at 400 F for 5 minutes more.
6. Serve and enjoy.

Nutrition: Calories 265 Fat 21.4 g Carbohydrates 11.9 g Sugar 2.4 g Protein 10.2 g Cholesterol 65 mg

2. Perfect Crispy Tofu

Preparation Time: 10 Minutes

Cooking Time: 20 Minutes

Servings: 4

Ingredients:

- 1 block firm tofu
- 1 tbsp arrowroot flour
- 2 tsp sesame oil
- 1 tsp vinegar
- 2 tbsp soy sauce

Directions:

1. In a bowl, toss tofu with oil, vinegar, and soy sauce and let sit for 15 minutes.
2. Toss marinated tofu with arrowroot flour.
3. Spray air fryer basket with cooking spray.
4. Add tofu in air fryer basket and cook for 20 minutes at 370 F. Shake basket halfway through.
5. Serve and enjoy.

Nutrition: Calories 42 Fat 0.5 g Carbohydrates 1.3 g Sugar 0.3g Protein 12.4 g Cholesterol 0 mg

3. Roasted Peppers

Preparation Time: 5 Minutes

Cooking Time: 8 Minutes

Servings: 3

Ingredients:

- 3 1/2 cups bell peppers, cut into chunks
- Pepper
- Salt

Directions:

1. Spray air fryer basket with cooking spray.
2. Add bell peppers into the air fryer basket and cook at 360 F for 8 minutes.
3. Season peppers with pepper and salt.
4. Serve and enjoy.

Nutrition: Calories 33 Fat 0 g Carbohydrates 7 g Sugar 4 g Protein 1 g Cholesterol 0 mg

MAINS: POULTRY

1. Crispy Southern Fried Chicken

Preparation Time: 10 Minutes

Cooking Time: 25 Minutes

Servings: 4

Ingredients:

- 1 tsp. cayenne pepper
- 2 tbsp. mustard powder
- 2 tbsp. oregano
- 2 tbsp. thyme
- 3 tbsp. coconut milk
- 1 beaten egg
- ¼ C. cauliflower
- ¼ C. gluten-free oats
- 8 chicken drumsticks

Directions:

1. Preparing the Ingredients. Ensure the Power air fryer XL is preheated to 350 degrees.
2. Lay out chicken and season with pepper and salt on all sides.
3. Add all other ingredients to a blender, blending till a smooth-like breadcrumb mixture is created.

Place in a bowl and add a beaten egg to another bowl.

4. Dip chicken into breadcrumbs, then into the egg, and breadcrumbs once more.

5. Air Frying. Place coated drumsticks into the Power air fryer XL. Set temperature to 350°F, and set time to 20 minutes and cook 20 minutes. Bump up the temperature to 390 degrees and cook another 5 minutes till crispy.

Nutrition: Calories: 504 Fat: 18g Protein: 35g Sugar: 5g

2. Tex-Mex Turkey Burgers

Preparation Time: 10 Minutes

Cooking Time: 15 Minutes

Servings: 4

Ingredients:

- 1/3 cup finely crushed corn tortilla chips
- 1 egg, beaten
- ¼ cup salsa
- 1/3 cup shredded pepper Jack cheese
- Pinch salt
- Freshly ground black pepper
- 1-pound ground turkey
- 1 tablespoon olive oil
- 1 teaspoon paprika

Directions:

1. Preparing the Ingredients. In a medium bowl, combine the tortilla chips, egg, salsa, cheese, salt, and pepper, and mix well.
2. Add the turkey and mix gently but thoroughly with clean hands.

3. Form the meat mixture into patties about ½ inch thick. Make an indentation in the center of each patty with your thumb, so the burgers don't puff up while cooking.
4. Brush the patties on both sides with the olive oil and sprinkle with paprika.
5. Air Frying. Put in the Power air fryer XL basket. Grill for 14 to 16 minutes or until the meat registers at least 165°F.

Nutrition: Calories: 354 Fat: 21g Protein: 36g Fiber: 2g

3. Air Fryer Turkey Breast

Preparation Time: 5 Minutes

Cooking Time: 60 Minutes

Servings: 6

Ingredients:

- Pepper and salt
- 1 oven-ready turkey breast
- Turkey seasonings of choice

Directions:

1. Preparing the Ingredients. Preheat the Power air fryer XL to 350 degrees.
2. Season turkey with pepper, salt, and other desired seasonings.
3. Place turkey in the Power air fryer XL basket.
4. Air Frying. Set temperature to 350°F, and set time to 60 minutes. Cook 60 minutes. The meat should be at 165 degrees when done.
5. Allow to rest 10-15 minutes before slicing. Enjoy!

Nutrition: Calories: 212 Fat: 12g Protein: 24g Sugar: 0g

4. Mustard Chicken Tenders

Preparation Time: 5 Minutes

Cooking Time: 20 Minutes

Servings: 4

Ingredients:

- ½ C. coconut flour
- 1 tbsp. spicy brown mustard
- 2 beaten eggs
- 1 pound of chicken tenders

Directions:

1. Preparing the Ingredients. Season tenders with pepper and salt.
2. Place a thin layer of mustard onto tenders and then dredge in flour and dip in egg.
3. Air Frying. Add to the Power air fryer XL, set temperature to 390°F, and set time to 20 minutes.

Nutrition: Calories: 403 Fat: 20g Protein: 22g Sugar: 4g

MAINS: PORK

1. Rustic Pork Ribs

Preparation Time: 5 Minutes

Cooking Time: 15 Minutes

Servings: 4

Ingredients:

- 1 rack of pork ribs
- 3 tablespoons dry red wine
- 1 tablespoon soy sauce
- 1/2 teaspoon dried thyme
- 1/2 teaspoon onion powder
- 1/2 teaspoon garlic powder
- 1/2 teaspoon ground black pepper
- 1 teaspoon smoke salt
- 1 tablespoon cornstarch
- 1/2 teaspoon olive oil

Directions:

1. Preparing the Ingredients. Begin by preheating your POWER air fryer to 390 degrees F. Place all

ingredients in a mixing bowl and let them marinate at least 1 hour.

2. Air Frying. Cook the marinated ribs approximately 25 minutes at 390 degrees F.

3. Serve hot.

Nutrition: Calories: 309 Fat: 11g Protein: 21g Sugar: 2g

2. Keto Parmesan Crusted Pork Chops

Preparation Time: 10 Minutes

Cooking Time: 15 Minutes

Servings: 8

Ingredients:

- 3 tbsp. grated parmesan cheese
- 1 C. pork rind crumbs
- 2 beaten eggs
- ¼ tsp. chili powder
- ½ tsp. onion powder
- 1 tsp. smoked paprika
- ¼ tsp. pepper
- ½ tsp. salt
- 4-6 thick boneless pork chops

Directions:

1. Preparing the Ingredients. Ensure your air fryer is preheated to 400 degrees.
2. With pepper and salt, season both sides of pork chops.

3. In a food processor, pulse pork rinds into crumbs. Mix crumbs with other seasonings. Beat eggs and add to another bowl.
4. Dip pork chops into eggs then into pork rind crumb mixture.
5. Air Frying. Spray down air fryer with olive oil and add pork chops to the basket. Set temperature to 400°F, and set time to 15 minutes.

Nutrition: Calories: 422 Fat: 19g Protein: 38g Sugar: 2g

3. Crispy Fried Pork Chops the Southern Way

Preparation Time: 10 Minutes

Cooking Time: 25 Minutes

Servings: 4

Ingredients:

- ½ cup all-purpose flour
- ½ cup low fat buttermilk
- ½ teaspoon black pepper
- ½ teaspoon Tabasco sauce
- teaspoon paprika
- 3 bone-in pork chops

Directions:

1. Preparing the Ingredients. Place the buttermilk and hot sauce in a Ziploc bag and add the pork chops. Allow to marinate for at least an hour in the fridge.
2. In a bowl, combine the flour, paprika, and black pepper.

3. Remove pork from the Ziploc bag and dredge in the flour mixture.
4. Preheat the air fryer to 390°F.
5. Spray the pork chops with cooking oil.
6. Air Frying. Place in the air fryer basket and cook for 25 minutes.

Nutrition: Calories: 427 Fat: 21.2g Protein: 46.4g Sugar: 2g

4. Pork Meatloaf

Preparation Time: 15 Minutes

Cooking Time: 1 Hour and 5 Minutes

Servings: 8

Ingredients:

- For Meatloaf:
- 2 pounds lean ground pork
- 1 cup quick-cooking oats
- ½ cup carrot, peeled and shredded
- 1 medium onion, chopped
- ½ cup fat-free milk
- ¼ of egg, beaten
- 2 tablespoons ketchup
- 1 teaspoon garlic powder
- ¼ teaspoon ground black pepper
- For Topping:
- ¼ cup ketchup
- ¼ cup quick-cooking oats

Directions:

1. For meatloaf: in a bowl, add all the ingredients and mix until well combined.

2. For topping: in another bowl, add all the ingredients and mix until well combined.
3. Transfer the mixture into a greased loaf pan and top with the topping mixture.
4. Press "Power Button" of Power XL Digital Air Fry Oven and turn the dial to select "Air Bake" mode.
5. Press "Time Button" and again turn the dial to set the cooking time to 65 minutes.
6. Now push "Temp Button" and rotate the dial to set the temperature at 350 degrees F.
7. Press "Start/Pause" button to start.
8. When the unit beeps to show that it is preheated, open the lid.
9. Arrange the loaf pan over the wire rack and insert in the oven.
10. When cooking time is complete, open the lid and place the loaf pan onto a wire rack for about 10 minutes.
11. Carefully invert the loaf onto the wire rack.
12. Cut into desired sized slices and serve.

Nutrition: Calories: 239 Fat: 9.1g Sat Fat: 2.7g Carbohydrates: 14.5gFiber: 1.8g Sugar: 4.5g Protein: 25.1g

SNACKS

1. Pork Stuffed Dumplings

Preparation Time: 15 Minutes

Cooking Time: 12 Minutes

Servings: 3

Ingredients:

- 1 tsp. canola oil
- 4 cups chopped book Choy
- 1 tbsp. chopped fresh ginger
- 1 tbsp. chopped garlic
- 4 oz. ground pork
- 1/4 tsp. crushed red pepper
- 18 dumpling wrappers
- Cooking spray
- 2 tbsp. rice vinegar
- 2 tsp. lower-sodium soy sauce
- 1 tsp. toasted sesame oil
- 1/2 tsp. packed light Sugar
- 1 tbsp. finely chopped scallions

Directions:

1. In a greased skillet, sauté bok choy for 8 minutes, then add ginger and garlic. Cook for 1 minute. Transfer the bok choy to a plate.
2. Add pork and red pepper then mix well. Place the dumpling wraps on the working surface and divide the pork fillings on the dumpling wraps.
3. Wet the edges of the wraps and pinch them together to seal the filling. Place the dumpling in the Air Fryer basket.
4. Set the Air Fryer basket inside the Air Fryer toaster oven and close the lid. Select the Air Fry mode at 375°F temperature for 12 minutes. Flip the dumplings after 6 minutes then resume cooking. Serve fresh.

Nutrition: Calories: 172 Cal Protein: 2.1 g Carbs: 18.6 g Fat: 10.7 g

2. Panko Tofu with Mayo Sauce

Preparation Time: 10 Minutes

Cooking Time: 20 Minutes

Servings: 4

Ingredients:

- 8 tofu cutlets
- For the Marinade
- 1 tbsp toasted sesame oil
- 1/4 cup soy sauce
- 1 tsp rice vinegar
- 1/2 tsp garlic powder
- 1 tsp. ground ginger
- Make the Tofu:
- 1/2 cup vegan mayo
- 1 cup panko breadcrumbs
- 1 tsp. of sea salt

Directions:

1. Whisk the marinade ingredients in a bowl and add tofu cutlets. Mix well to coat the cutlets. Cover and marinate for 1 hour.

2. Meanwhile, whisk crumbs with salt and mayo in a bowl. Coat the cutlets with crumbs mixture. Place the tofu cutlets in the Air Fryer basket. Set the basket inside the Air Fryer toaster oven and close the lid.
3. Select the Air Fry mode at 370°F temperature for 20 minutes. Flip the cutlets after 10 minutes then resume cooking. Serve warm.

Nutrition: Calories: 151 Cal Protein: 1.9 g Carbs: 6.9 g Fat: 8.6 g

3. Garlicky Bok Choy

Preparation Time: 10 Minutes

Cooking Time: 10 Minutes

Servings: 2

Ingredients:

- 4 bunches baby book Choy
- Spray oil
- 1 tsp. garlic powder

Directions:

1. Toss bok choy with garlic powder and spread them in the Air Fryer basket.
2. Spray them with cooking oil. Place the basket inside the Air Fryer toaster oven and close the lid. Select the Air Fry mode at 350°F temperature for 6 minutes. Serve fresh.

Nutrition: Calories: 81 Cal Protein: 0.4 g Carbs: 4.7 g Fat: 8.3 g

4. Seasoned Cauliflower Chunks

Preparation Time: 10 Minutes

Cooking Time: 15 Minutes

Servings: 4

Ingredients:

- 1 cauliflower head, diced into chunks
- ½ cup unsweetened milk
- 6 tbsp. mayo
- ¼ cup all-purpose flour
- ¾ cup almond meal
- ¼ cup almond meal
- 1 tsp. onion powder
- 1 tsp. garlic powder
- 1 tsp. of sea salt
- ½ tsp. paprika
- Pinch of black pepper
- Cooking oil spray

Directions:

1. Toss cauliflower with rest of the ingredients in a bowl then transfers to the Air Fryer basket. Spray them with cooking oil.
2. Set the basket inside the Air Fryer toaster oven and close the lid. Select the Air Fry mode at 400°F temperature for 15 minutes. Toss well and serve warm.

Nutrition: Calories: 137 Cal Protein: 6.1 g Carbs: 26 g Fat: 8 g

5. Tofu Popcorns

Preparation Time: 15 Minutes

Cooking Time: 15 Minutes

Servings: 4

Ingredients:

- 2 cups tofu, diced
- 3 ¾ cups vegetable broth, divided
- 2 garlic cloves, mashed
- 1 tsp. salt
- 1-inch cube ginger, grated
- ½ cup all-purpose flour
- ½ cup of corn starch
- 1 cup panko breadcrumbs
- 1 tbsp. garlic powder
- 1 tbsp. lemon pepper
- ½ tsp. salt

Directions:

1. Toss tofu with ginger, salt, and garlic in a large bowl. Pour in 3 cups of broth and soak or 20 minutes.

2. Whisk wheat flour with cornstarch and ¾ cup broth in a bowl until smooth. Remove the tofu cubes from the milk and dip the cubes in the flour batter.
3. Place the tofu chunks in the Air Fryer basket. Set the basket inside the Air Fryer toaster oven and close the lid. Select the Air Fry mode at 390°F temperature for 15 minutes. Serve fresh.

Nutrition: Calories: 110 Cal Protein: 2.7 g Carbs: 12.8g Fat: 1.9 g

6. Puerto Rican Tostones

Preparation Time: 5 Minutes

Cooking Time: 15 Minutes

Servings: 2

Ingredients:

- One ripe plantain, sliced
- One tablespoon sunflower oil
- A pinch of grated nutmeg
- A pinch of kosher salt

Directions:

1. Toss the plantains with the oil, nutmeg, and salt in a bowl.
2. Cook in the preheated Air Fryer at 400 degrees F for 10 minutes, shaking the cooking basket halfway through the cooking time.
3. Regulate the seasonings to taste and serve immediately.

Nutrition: Calories 151 Fat 1g Carbs 29g Protein 6g Sugar 17g

SIDES

1. Scrambled Eggs

Preparation Time: 5 Minutes

Cooking Time: 15 Minutes

Servings: 2

Ingredients:

- 2 tbsp. olive oil, melted
- eggs, whisked
- oz. fresh spinach, chopped
- 1 medium-sized tomato, chopped
- 1 tsp. fresh lemon juice
- ½ tsp. coarse salt
- ½ tsp. ground black pepper
- ½ cup of fresh basil, roughly chopped

Directions:

1. Grease the Air Fryer baking pan with the oil, tilting it to spread the oil around. Pre-heat the fryer at 280degreesF.

2. Mix the remaining ingredients, apart from the basil leaves, whisking well until everything is completely combined.
3. Cook in the fryer for 8 - 12 minutes.
4. Top with fresh basil leaves before serving with little sour cream if desired.

Nutrition: Calories: 140 Fat: 10g Carbs: 2g Protein: 12g

2. Bacon-Wrapped Onion Rings

Preparation Time: 10 Minutes

Cooking Time: 15 Minutes

Servings: 8

Ingredients:

- 1 large onion, peeled
- slices sugar-free bacon
- 1 tbsp. sriracha

Directions:

1. Chop up the onion into slices a quarter-inch thick. Gently pull apart the rings. Take a slice of bacon and wrap it around an onion ring. Repeat with the rest of the ingredients.
2. Place each onion ring in your fryer.
3. Cut the onion rings at 350degreesF for ten minutes, turning them halfway through to ensure the bacon crisps up.
4. Serve hot with the sriracha.

Nutrition: Calories: 280 Fat: 19g Carbs: 25g Protein: 3g

3. Grilled Cheese

Preparation Time: 5 Minutes

Cooking Time: 25 Minutes

Servings: 2

Ingredients:

- 4 slices of bread
- ½ cup sharp cheddar cheese
- ¼ cup butter, melted

Directions:

1. Pre-heat the Air Fryer at 360degreesF.
2. Put cheese and butter in separate bowls.
3. Apply the butter to each side of the bread slices with a brush.
4. Spread the cheese across two of the slices of bread and make two sandwiches. Transfer both to the fryer.
5. Cook for 5 – 7 minutes or until a golden-brown color is achieved and the cheese is melted.

Nutrition: Calories: 170 Fat: 8g Carbs: 17g Protein: 5g

4. Peppered Puff Pastry

Preparation Time: 10 Minutes

Cooking Time: 25 Minutes

Servings: 4

Ingredients:

- 1 ½ tbsp. sesame oil
- 1 cup white mushrooms, sliced
- 2 cloves garlic, minced
- 1 bell pepper, seeded and chopped
- ¼ tsp. sea salt
- ¼ tsp. dried rosemary
- ½ tsp. ground black pepper, or more to taste
- oz. puff pastry sheets
- ½ cup crème fraiche
- 1 egg, well whisked
- ½ cup parmesan cheese, preferably freshly grated

Directions:

1. Pre-heat your Air Fryer to 400degreesF.
2. Heat the sesame oil over moderate temperature and fry the mushrooms, garlic, and pepper until soft and fragrant.

3. Sprinkle on the salt, rosemary, and pepper.
4. In the meantime, unroll the puff pastry and slice it into 4-inch squares.
5. Spread the crème fraiche across each square.
6. Spoon equal amounts of the vegetables into the puff pastry squares. Enclose each square around the filling in triangle shape, pressing the edges with your fingertips.
7. Brush each triangle with some whisked egg and cover with grated Parmesan.
8. Cook for 22-25 minutes.

Nutrition: Calories: 259 Fat: 18g Carbs: 21g Protein: 3g

5. Horseradish Mayo & Gorgonzola Mushrooms

Preparation Time: 10 Minutes

Cooking Time: 15 Minutes

Servings: 5

Ingredients:

- ½ cup of breadcrumbs
- 2 cloves garlic, pressed
- 2 tbsp. fresh coriander, chopped
- 1/3 tsp. kosher salt
- ½ tsp. crushed red pepper flakes
- 1 ½ tbsp. olive oil
- 2 medium-sized mushrooms, stems removed
- ½ cup Gorgonzola cheese, grated
- ¼ cup low-fat mayonnaise
- 1 tsp. prepared horseradish, well-drained
- 1 tbsp. fresh parsley, finely chopped

Directions:

1. Combine the breadcrumbs together with the garlic, coriander, salt, red pepper, and the olive oil.
2. Take equal-sized amounts of the bread crumb mixture and use them to stuff the mushroom caps. Add the grated Gorgonzola on top of each.
3. Put the mushrooms in the Air Fryer grill pan and transfer to the fryer.
4. Grill them at 380degreesF for 8-12 minutes, ensuring the stuffing is warm throughout.
5. In the meantime, prepare the horseradish mayo. Mix together the mayonnaise, horseradish and parsley.
6. When the mushrooms are ready, serve with the mayo.

Nutrition: Calories: 140 Fat: 13g Carbs: 6g Protein: 0g

6. Crumbed Beans

Preparation Time: 5 Minutes

Cooking Time: 10 Minutes

Servings: 4

Ingredients:

- ½ cup flour
- 1 tsp. smoky chipotle powder
- ½ tsp. ground black pepper
- 1 tsp. sea salt flakes
- 2 eggs, beaten
- ½ cup crushed saltines
- 20 oz. wax beans

Directions:

1. Combine the flour, chipotle powder, black pepper, and salt in a bowl. Put the eggs in second bowl. Place the crushed saltines in third bowl.
2. Wash the beans with cold water and discard any tough strings.

3. Coat the beans with the flour mixture, before dipping them into the beaten egg. Lastly cover them with the crushed saltines.

4. Spritz the beans with cooking spray.

5. Air-fry at 360degreesF for 4 minutes. Give the cooking basket a good shake and continue to cook for 3 minutes. Serve hot.

Nutrition: Calories: 200 Fat: 8g Carbs: 27g Protein: 4g

7. Bok Choy and Butter Sauce

Preparation Time: 5 Minutes

Cooking Time: 20 Minutes

Servings: 4

Ingredients:

- Two bok choy heads; trimmed and cut into strips
- 1 tbsp. butter; melted
- 2 tbsp. chicken stock
- 1 tsp. lemon juice
- 1 tbsp. olive oil

Directions:

1. Mix all the ingredients, toss, introduce the pan to the air fryer, then cook at 380°F for 15 minutes.
2. Split between plates and serve as a side dish

Nutrition: Calories: 141 Fat: 3g Fiber: 2g Carbs: 4g Protein: 3g

8. Turmeric Mushroom

Preparation Time: 5 Minutes

Cooking Time: 20 Minutes

Servings: 4

Ingredients:

- 1 lb. brown mushrooms
- Four garlic cloves; minced
- ¼ tsp. cinnamon powder
- 1 tsp. olive oil
- ½ tsp. turmeric powder

Directions:

1. Mix all the fixings and toss.
2. Put the mushrooms in your air fryer's basket and cook at 370°F for 15 minutes
3. Divide the mix between plates and serve as a side dish.

Nutrition: Calories: 208 Fat: 7g Fiber: 3g Carbs: 5g Protein: 7g

DESSERT

1. Blueberry Coconut Crackers

Preparation Time: 10 Minutes

Cooking Time: 30 Minutes

Servings: 12

Ingredients:

- ½ cup coconut butter
- ½ cup coconut oil, melted
- 1 cup blueberries
- 3tablespoons coconut sugar

Directions:

1. In a pot that fits your air fryer, mix coconut butter with coconut oil, raspberries and sugar, toss, introduce in the fryer and cook at 367 degrees F for 30 minutes
2. Spread on a lined baking sheet, keep in the fridge for a few hours, slice crackers and serve.
3. Enjoy!

Nutrition: Calories: 174 Protein: 7 g. Fat: 5 g. Carbs: 4 g.

2. Cauliflower Pudding

Preparation Time: 10 Minutes

Cooking Time: 30 Minutes

Servings: 4

Ingredients:

- 2½ cups water
- 1 cup coconut sugar
- 2cups cauliflower rice
- 2cinnamon sticks
- ½ cup coconut, shredded

Directions:

1. In a pot that fits your air fryer, mix water with coconut sugar, cauliflower rice, cinnamon and coconut, stir, introduce in the fryer and cook at 365 degrees F for 30 minutes
2. Divide pudding into cups and serve cold.
3. Enjoy!

Nutrition: Calories: 203 Protein: 4 g. Fat: 4 g. Carbs: 9 g.

3. Sweet Vanilla Rhubarb

Preparation Time: 10 Minutes

Cooking Time: 10 Minutes

Servings: 4

Ingredients:

- 5 cups rhubarb, chopped
- 2 tablespoons coconut butter, melted
- 1/3 cup water
- 1 tablespoon stevia
- 1 teaspoon vanilla extract

Directions:

1. Put rhubarb, ghee, water, stevia and vanilla extract in a pan that fits your air fryer, introduce in the fryer and cook at 365 degrees F for 10 minutes
2. Divide into small bowls and serve cold.
3. Enjoy!

Nutrition: Calories: 103 Protein: 2 g. Fat: 2 g. Carbs: 6 g.

4. Pineapple Pudding

Preparation Time: 10 Minutes

Cooking Time: 5 Minutes

Servings: 8

Ingredients:

- 1 tablespoon avocado oil
- 1 cup rice
- 14ounces milk
- Sugar to the taste
- 8ounces canned pineapple, chopped

Directions:

1. In your air fryer, mix oil, milk and rice, stir, cover and cook on High for 3 minutes.
2. Add sugar and pineapple, stir, cover and cook on High for 2 minutes more.
3. Divide into dessert bowls and serve.

Nutrition: Calories: 154 Protein: 8 g. Fat: 4 g. Carbs: 14 g.

5. Coconut Pancake

Preparation Time: 10 Minutes

Cooking Time: 20 Minutes

Servings: 4

Ingredients:

- 2 cups self-rising flour
- 2 tablespoons sugar
- 2 eggs
- 1 and ½ cups coconut milk
- A drizzle of olive oil

Directions:

1. In a bowl, mix eggs with sugar, milk and flour and whisk until you obtain a batter.
2. Grease your air fryer with the oil, add the batter, spread into the pot, cover and cook on Low for 20 minutes.
3. Slice pancake, divide between plates and serve cold.

Nutrition: Calories: 162 Protein: 8 g. Fat: 3 g. Carbs: 7 g.

6. Cinnamon Rolls

Preparation Time: 2 Hours

Cooking Time: 15 Minutes

Servings: 8

Ingredients:

- 1-pound vegan bread dough
- ¾ cup coconut sugar
- 1 and ½ tablespoons cinnamon powder
- 2tablespoons vegetable oil

Directions:

1. Roll dough on a floured working surface, shape a rectangle and brush with the oil.
2. In a bowl, mix cinnamon with sugar, stir, sprinkle this over dough, roll into a log, seal well and cut into 8 pieces.
3. Leave rolls to rise for 2 hours, place them in your air fryer's basket, cook at 350 degrees F for 5 minutes, flip them, cook for 4 minutes more and transfer to a platter.
4. Enjoy!

Nutrition: Calories: 170 Protein: 6 g. Fat: 1 g. Carbs: 7 g.

7. Strawberry Cheesecake Chimichangas

Preparation Time: 15 Minutes

Cooking Time: 10 Minutes

Servings: 6

Ingredients:

- 6 (8-inch) soft flour tortillas
- 8 ounces cream cheese
- Two tablespoons sour cream
- One teaspoon vanilla extract
- 3/4 cups strawberries

Directions:

1. Allow the cream cheese to soften and slice your strawberries into thin slices.
2. Beat together cream cheese, vanilla, sugar, and sour cream.
3. Fold the strawberries into the mixture.
4. Spread the filling on the bottom 1/3 of each tortilla.
5. Fold the bottom and top of the tortilla in, then roll it up from the sides.

6. Cook at 340 for about 8 minutes or until the tortillas become crisp.

7. Allow cooling a few minutes before serving.

Nutrition: Calories: 296 Sodium: 574 mg Dietary Fiber: 5.4g Fat: 18.1g Carbs: 27.7g Protein: 8.1g

CONCLUSION

Congratulations on having reached the end of this culinary journey with the help of our beloved Power XL air fryer.

I hope you enjoyed cooking with this incredible tool, making healthy and tasty dishes without using excessive oil or butter.

You can have fun creating completely new recipes taking inspiration from the ones you found in this cookbook!

It doesn't take much, just a lot of creativity, a lot of passion for cooking and the Power XL!

I am sure you will create tasty and innovative dishes.

I wish you good luck!

Good luck!

CPSIA information can be obtained
at www.ICGtesting.com
Printed in the USA
BVHW080759140521
607270BV00006B/962